ODD SCIENCE
INCREDIBLE CREATURES

James Olstein

STERLING CHILDREN'S BOOKS

New York

Creatures are fascinating, from miniscule bugs to great beasts of the deep, from ferocious dinosaurs to cute-looking pandas.

The natural world has all kinds of strange secrets you do not know—such as birds that roost in the armpits of giraffes, spiders that strum the strings of their webs like a guitar, and screaming shrimp—one of the loudest creatures on Earth.

This book will reveal things you have never heard of before. It will tell you unknown facts about the creatures that you do know, and it will surprise you with weird and wonderful creatures that you don't.

This book will tell you why your dog might not recognize you on screen, how penguins "propose" to one another, and which came first between the chicken and the egg.

Quirky, strange, and cool—come inside the world of odd science.

———

For little Jimmy.
You were just a little creature in your mom's belly
when I made this.

CONTENTS

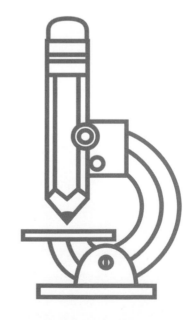

DINO-MITE

Scientists believe that the birds we know are descended from theropods (two-legged dinosaurs, such as *T. rex* and the *Velociraptors*). As they evolved, they became smaller, which has been an advantage for them, because they could avoid predators. Over time, they shrunk until they have become the size of modern birds.

SLAM DUNK

Some dinosaur eggs were as big as basketballs.

BABY LOVE

Scientists have discovered that the skulls of young dinosaurs have much bigger eyes and features compared to adults. This made the little creatures look much cuter and more lovable than their parents.

NOW YOU SEE ME . . .

The fossil of the *Psittacosaurus* (parrot lizard) reveals a clever type of camouflage called countershading. Its body had a light underside and dark top, making it look flatter and harder to see.

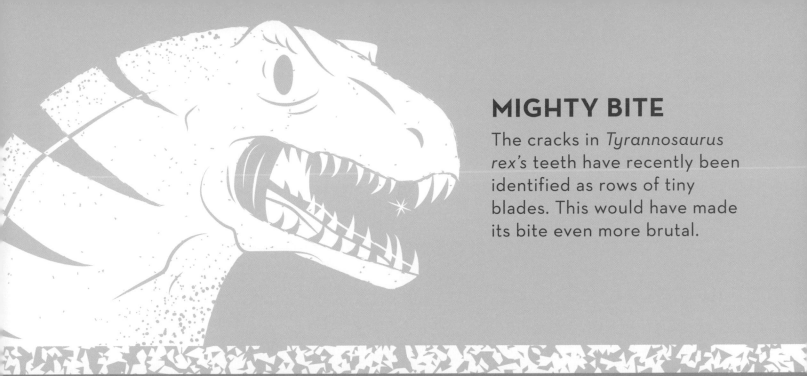

MIGHTY BITE

The cracks in *Tyrannosaurus rex*'s teeth have recently been identified as rows of tiny blades. This would have made its bite even more brutal.

FLOSS-A-RAPTOR

When studied under a microscope, hadrosaurs were found to have an astonishing number of teeth. Each duck-billed dino fossil had around 300 pearly whites.

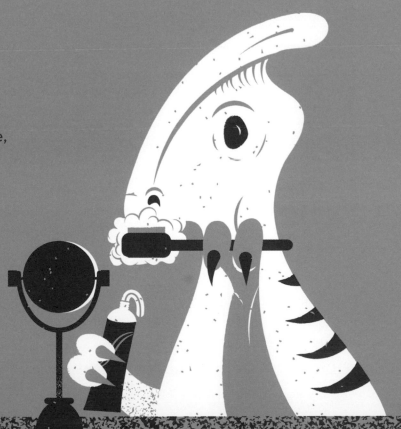

SHORE THING

Scientists have found dinosaur footprints on the Isle of Skye, in Scotland, that suggest they may have enjoyed a swim. It appears that sauropods frequently made trips to beaches and other bodies of water.

SOUND SYSTEM

Some sauropods may have been able to swing their tails hard enough to create a sonic boom. Each flick was so fast it could have exceeded 750 miles per hour.

READY FOUR TAKE OFF

It is believed that the first flying dinosaurs evolved four wings. Species such as the *Microraptor gui* may have used two extra hind wings and a long tail to help them soar.

PEAK PREDATOR

The *Dakotaraptor* not only had hook claws on its feet like a regular raptor, they also sprung out of its hands. This made it an excellent climber and predator.

F-F-FROSTY!

Scientists have discovered a new breed of dinosaur that once roamed the Arctic. *Ugrunaaluk kuukpikensis* (Inuit for "ancient grazer") was a plant-eating dinosaur able to survive in cold weather.

TIME TO FLY

Some mammals during the Jurassic period had wing-like skin membranes that enabled them to glide from tree to tree, high above the dinosaurs.

LETTUCE EAT

The vast majority
of dinosaurs were
vegetarians . . .

NO MISSED STEAK

. . . *Tyrannosaurus rex,*
however, gobbled up to
24.5 tons of meat
a year.

BACK TO THE GRIND

It is thought that dinosaurs deliberately ate rocks. The rocks churned inside each creature's stomach, helping to break down food. Today's crocodiles do the same thing.

EGGS-ACTLY

We know that dinosaurs hatched from eggs, but how did their parents keep the nest warm without cracking them? Scientists studying the oviraptorosaurs discovered that these dinosaurs would stack their eggs in a circle to distribute the pressure being put on them, while still keeping them protected.

BIG BUDDY, LITTLE BUDDY

The largest known dinosaur is the *Argentinosaurus*. It lived during the Cretaceous period and was an estimated 130 feet long. Scientists believe its weight could have been as much as 110 tons. One of the smallest dinosaurs was the *Microraptor*, which was just 2 feet 7½ inches long and weighed 2 pounds 3 ounces.

BONE-A-FIDE

The *Tyrannosaurus rex* and the *Velociraptor* both had wishbones, just like a turkey.

DINO DISPLAY

When miners in Canada came across the remains of a nodosaur, the dinosaur was so well preserved it looked like a sculpture rather than a fossil.

WHALE SCALE

The blue whale is the largest animal ever known to live on Earth. This ocean colossus can stretch up to 100 feet in length, and weigh up to 220 tons.

WHALE-Y USEFUL

Scientists have discovered a 30-million-year-old whale that used its teeth to both bite prey and filter seawater for food.

WHALE, HI THERE!

When humpback whales leap into the air and then slap back down into the water, they are sending an "acoustic telegram." The breaching noise is used to communicate with far-off groups of whales. It travels better than whale song.

JAW-SOME

Sharks have been lurking in the oceans for more than 400 million years. Even dinosaurs did not make an appearance until 230 million years ago. Some ancient sharks were massive, dwarfing the species that have evolved today.

NO FILTER

The basking shark eats anything that swims in its mouth. Its esophagus, or gullet, is closed, stopping seawater from entering its stomach.

WATER MUSIC

A documentary film crew learned that sharks are attracted to Death Metal music. When played underwater, the music sounds similar to noises made by struggling fish. Sharks are able to feel the vibrations through sensors that extend along the body.

TURTLE POWER

After the dinosaurs, there came a new kind of beast—the turtle. Scientists have found the remains of a giant species that lived in South America. The turtle was so enormous, it is believed to have fed primarily on crocodiles.

SEA YOU LATER

As soon as they are born, baby sea turtles swim out into the ocean. They spend up to 15 years floating on giant seaweed beds, drifting on the open sea. This time in the life of a turtle remains a mystery to scientists.

GHOST OF THE DEEP

A curious being floats along the ocean floor near Hawaii. The ghost octopus is a mysterious white creature without any pigment in its skin. It has been sighted at lower depths than any other octopus—more than $2^2/3$ miles below the surface.

BIG EYE

The colossal squid has an eye the size of a dinner plate At about 11 inches wide, these are the biggest peepers of any living animal. Scientists think the squid's eye evolved this way to help it see better in deep water.

JAWS TOO

Moray eels have a second set of jaws tucked away inside their throats. When a moray sees some prey, the extra teeth fire forward, dragging the victim down into its mouth.

AIR HAIR

The axolotl is a breed of salamander that always seems to be smiling. It also appears to have wild, feathery hair. The cute appendages are actually gills that it uses to breathe underwater.

CLAWS AND EFFECT

The mantis shrimp has the fastest
punch on the planet. Its claws are so
light and hard it can throw a punch
at 50 miles per hour.

SNAPPY SOUND

Small does not mean silent—
snapping shrimp are one of
the loudest animals in the
world. They create intense
"screams" by releasing air
bubbles from their claws.

BIRTHDAY FISHES

With some fish you can tell a specimen's age by counting the rings on its scales, like counting the rings inside a tree trunk.

THAT STINKS

The mandarinfish has no scales. It has a thick coating of smelly, bitter mucus instead. The fish's unusual skin is bright and colorful, warning would-be predators to stay away.

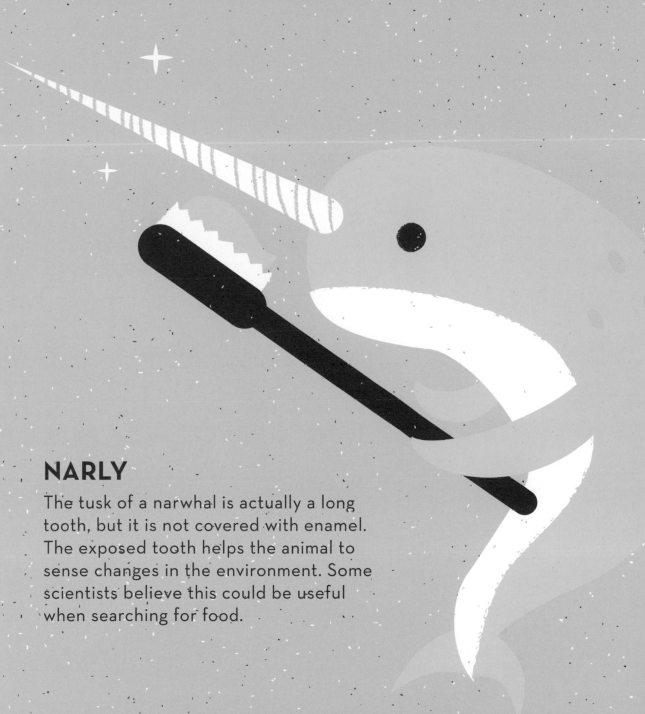

NARLY

The tusk of a narwhal is actually a long tooth, but it is not covered with enamel. The exposed tooth helps the animal to sense changes in the environment. Some scientists believe this could be useful when searching for food.

NAME GAME

Dolphins call out to each other by name. These "names" are distinct signature whistles that young dolphins develop as they grow up.

BRIAN THE SPIDER

A newly discovered species of Australian spider can float on water. The canny arachnid senses the tiny vibrations that bugs make as they move along. Once it finds a victim, it drags its meal down below the surface. The spider is named after a professor called Brian Greene.

SPIDER RIDER

In Japan, there is a parasitic wasp that lays its egg onto the back of orb weaver spiders. When the egg hatches, the larva rides on the spider's back, making it do its bidding.

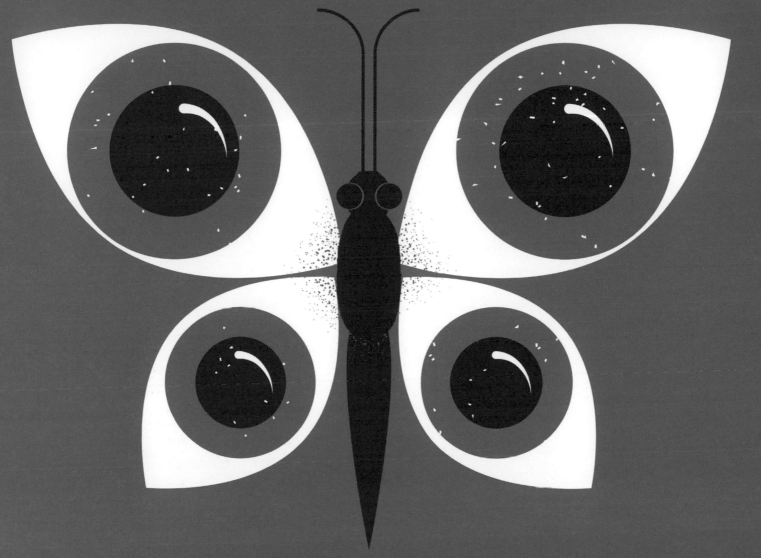

DOUBLE VISION

Butterflies have two kinds of eyes: a simple set that primarily detects changes in light and a compound set made up of 6,000 lenses that can see ultraviolet light. The patterns on their wings also sometimes resemble eyes—this is a form of camouflage that the butterfly uses to defend itself from predators. These patterns resemble the eyes of a number of deadly foes, such as owls and snakes.

BUZZ BUZZ

It is not just adult humans that enjoy caffeine.
Some flower nectar contains small doses of
caffeine. When bees visit these plants, they get
an energy boost similar to a coffee buzz.

NATURAL LIGHT

When living things produce their own light, it is called bioluminescence. The Brazilian railroad worm is a great example. It has a light on its head and more dotted along the sides of its body.

NO LIGHT MEAL

Fireflies do not light up for fun. Their glowing bodies help attract mates and let hungry animals know that they taste disgusting.

SPIDER SONGS

Spiders strum silk threads, just like the strings on a guitar. The sound the threads make carries information about food, mates, and the strength of their web.

HEAD TURNER

The praying mantis can turn its own head around by 180 degrees so it can see what is going on behind it.

DRUMMING UP FRIENDS

Male cockatoos in Australia like to keep a beat. The birds fashion tiny drumsticks out of branches, then tap out a tune. Each cockatoo plays its own unique rhythm, putting on a performance for watching females.

BIRD FOOD

Hummingbirds burn so much energy they need to consume the equivalent of their bodyweight in food every single day.

HEAD BANGER

A woodpecker can hit a tree with its beak at 1,000 times the force of gravity. Tiny platelike bones in the bird's skull form a natural helmet, protecting its brain from damage. It also has a third inner eyelid to stop its eyeball from popping out.

LOOK AT THE UPSIDE

The white-breasted nuthatch uses its hind big toes to hang upside down from tree branches.

BIRD BRAIN

Despite popular belief, the extinct dodo may actually have been smart. After scanning the bird's skull, scientists found that its brain was large compared to its body size.

HIGH RISE

Yellow-billed oxpeckers roost on giraffes when they go to sleep at night. They often settle in the giraffe's armpit.

TEARDROPS

A species of moth in Madagascar sneaks up on resting birds and then drinks their tears.

DENTAL TWEETMENT

Egyptian plover birds clean the teeth of crocodiles in exchange for the extra food.

45

CHICKEN WINNER

British researchers have come to the conclusion that the chicken came before the egg. The protein needed to make an eggshell can be found only inside a chicken's body.

COOL GIRLS

A baby alligator's gender is determined by the temperature of the nest. Eggs laid in bright, sunlit places will probably be male. Eggs that are incubated in a cool, shady nest will result in a clutch of baby girls.

HAVE AN ICE TRIP

Penguins have evolved to become such strong swimmers they can be found in different continents and countries besides Antarctica. There are now penguin colonies in Argentina, Australia, Ecuador, and South Africa.

ROCKY RELATIONSHIP

Gentoo penguins "propose" to potential mates by presenting them with rocks. Males will often fight to claim the smoothest pebbles to give.

SOUND OFF!

Although penguins do not have noticeable ears, they do have excellent hearing. This lets them communicate across great distances.

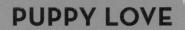

PUPPY LOVE

Prairie dogs kiss when they greet each other.
Researchers have found they kiss more when
they are being watched.

WE NEED EACH OTTER

Sea otters hold hands with their mates while sleeping so they do not float apart and drift away.

FUR REAL

The densest fur of any mammal is found on the sea otter. Their coats can grow up to one million hairs per square inch.

SLOW CAMO

Sloths have a symbiotic relationship with algae. The algae feeds off the moisture in the sloth's fur, but in exchange it provides camouflage from predators and extra nutrients that the sloth absorbs through its skin.

MAKE A SPLASH

Although they are slow on land, sloths are excellent swimmers.

HANGING OUT

Sloths spend most of their time hanging around in trees, but they do come down once a week to use the bathroom.

MONKEY BUSINESS

Chimpanzees are known to use tools, often made from stones or branches. Some even have a "tool kit" that they select items from to dig, drill, probe, or fish.

LEAF LIFE

Orangutans in Asia have been seen using leaves as napkins, gloves, and even shelter when it rains.

PURRFECT SOUND

Elephants purr in the same way that cats do, using it as a means of communication.

STRONG SMELLER

The Asian elephant has 150,000 muscle units in its trunk—that is some nose. The trunk is able to uproot trees, lift heavy objects, and spray a gallon of water.

POO MOUNTAIN

Elephants produce enough poo in seven hours to outweigh a grown-up human.

THERE'S NO PLACE LIKE HOME

Some frog species find warmth and shelter living in piles of elephant dung.

A BEAR FOR ALL SEASONS

Biologists believe that pandas have black-and-white markings because they do not hibernate. The two-color pelt allows for the bears to be camouflaged in both summer and winter.

BAMBOOZLED

Pandas fall asleep whenever and wherever they want to. They do not have to worry about predators, leaving them free to nap anytime they like.

HAND IT TO 'EM

Red pandas and giant pandas have evolved an extra thumblike digit to help them climb and eat.

POLAR EXPRESS

When it needs to, the polar bear can be swift in the snow. Running in short bursts, it can reach speeds of 25 miles per hour.

BACK SCRATCHER

Besides their ferocious growls, grizzly bears have another way they communicate—with scent. When a bear scratches its back against a tree, it is not only trying to relieve an itch. The bear is leaving its scent to "talk" to other bears—to find a partner or establish its territory.

CAT-COPHONY

Dogs can make ten distinct sounds when they bark and howl. Cats can make more than a hundred.

SOUND OFF

House cats can purr, but they cannot roar. Other cats, such as lions, tigers, leopards, and jaguars can roar, but they cannot purr.

PAY ATTENTION RIGHT MEOW

Studies show that cats prefer human companionship to eating food.

SOUR PUSS

Cats cannot taste sugar—unlike most other mammals, they do not have the ability to taste sweetness.

NO FLIES ON ME

Biologists disagree about the zebra's black-and-white stripes.
There are a lot of theories about the markings, but their most
probable purpose is thought to be deterring biting flies.

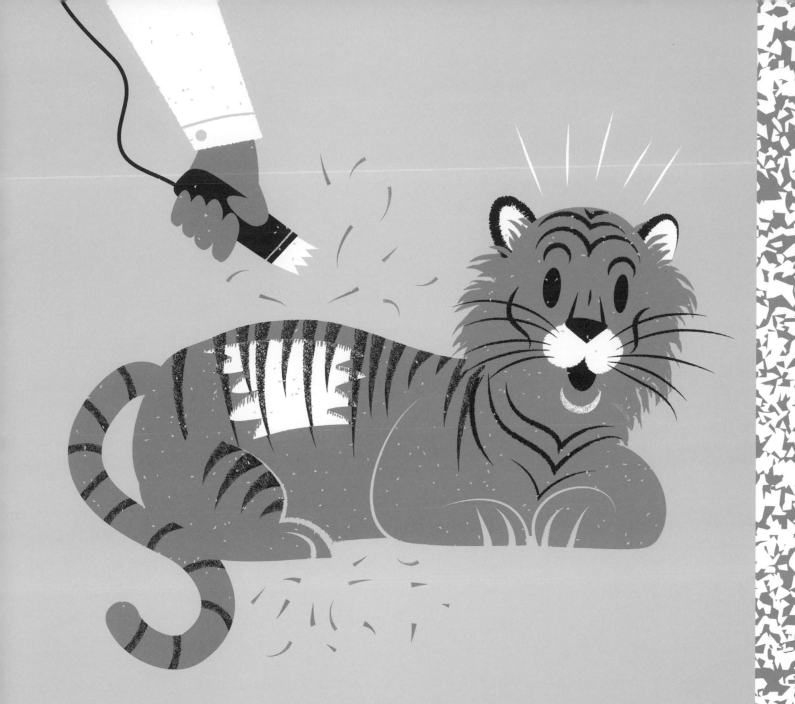

STRIPES FOREVER

If you shaved a tiger, you'd find that it has stripes on its skin, too. However, we do not recommend you try it.

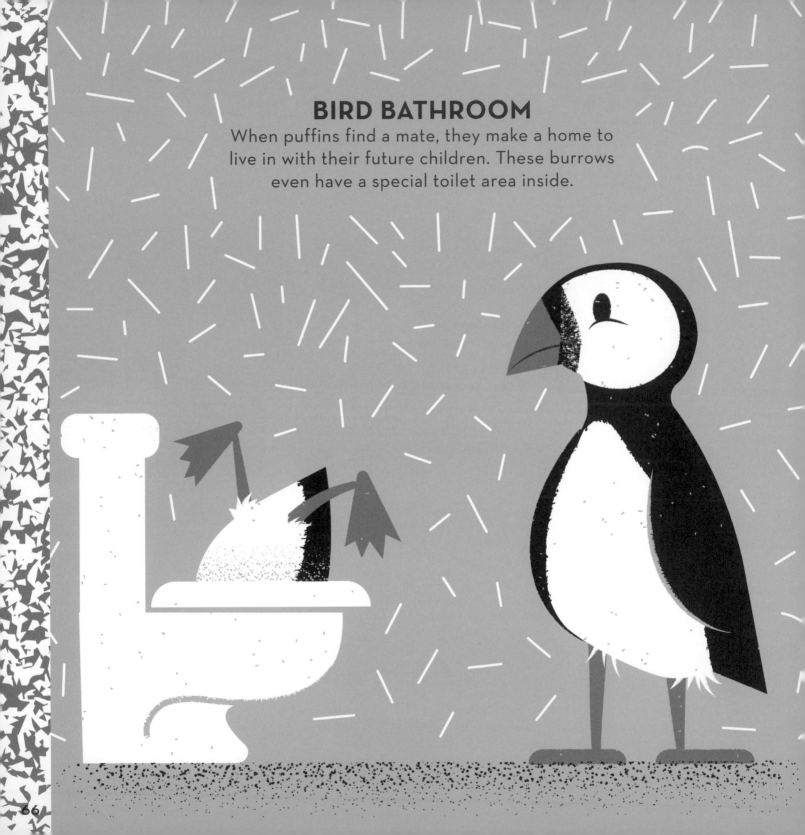

BIRD BATHROOM

When puffins find a mate, they make a home to live in with their future children. These burrows even have a special toilet area inside.

ANT-CIDENT

A species of ant in southeast Asia can make itself explode to help defend its colony. As it dies, the ant releases a sticky, toxic fluid from its abdomen.

RED FOR DANGER

When in danger, the regal horned lizard fights back by squirting nasty-tasting blood out of its eyes.

EAT YOUR GREENS

Most green birds get their color from the light refracted off their feathers.
The white-cheeked turaco, however, produces its own true green. The
pigment comes from copper absorbed from its fruit-heavy diet.

SHADY WATERS

Lake Hillier, in Western Australia, is entirely pink. The hue is created by the salt-loving algae that grows in it.

PRETTY IN PINK

Flamingos are born white. The mollusks, fish, and other food they eat make their feathers turn pink over time.

LOOSE NUTS

Every year, gray squirrels are responsible for planting thousands of trees. They forget where they stored their nuts, allowing for them to germinate instead.

PRETTY COO

Scientists in Tokyo have trained pigeons to distinguish between art styles. They can tell the difference between works by Picasso and Monet.

THAT'S RUFF

Dogs struggle to recognize people's faces when they appear on electronic tablets or smart phone screens. The small size and lack of human scent confuses them.

DOG FISH

Piranhas are able to croak, click, and even bark at their enemies.

BAT BANTER

The greater bulldog bat is one of the loudest mammals alive. Its cry is so high pitched that humans cannot even hear it.

WELL, THAT'S HAWK-WARD

Some smart blue jays can mimic the calls of hawks to scare off other birds.

GOT IT LICKED

A chameleon can flick out its tongue at dizzying speed. The tongue unravels telescopically, extending to twice the chameleon's body length, enabling it to catch a snack while remaining camouflaged.

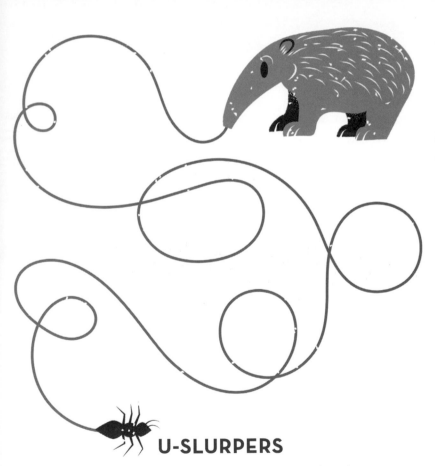

U-SLURPERS

Anteaters do not have any teeth—they use their long tongues to slurp up the ants that they find.

TER-MIGHTY FAST

The cheetah is a speedy sprinter (running at up to 74 miles per hour), but the tiny termite can move its jaws even faster. Some species can close their jaws so fast (more than 150 miles per hour), they can deliver a deathblow to any bug trespassing in the nest.

SPEED OF FLIGHT

When diving for prey, the peregrine falcon can reach dizzying speeds of 200 miles per hour.

FLEA THE SCENE

When a jumping flea leaps, its acceleration (more than 8,700 miles per hour) is faster than even a space shuttle launch.

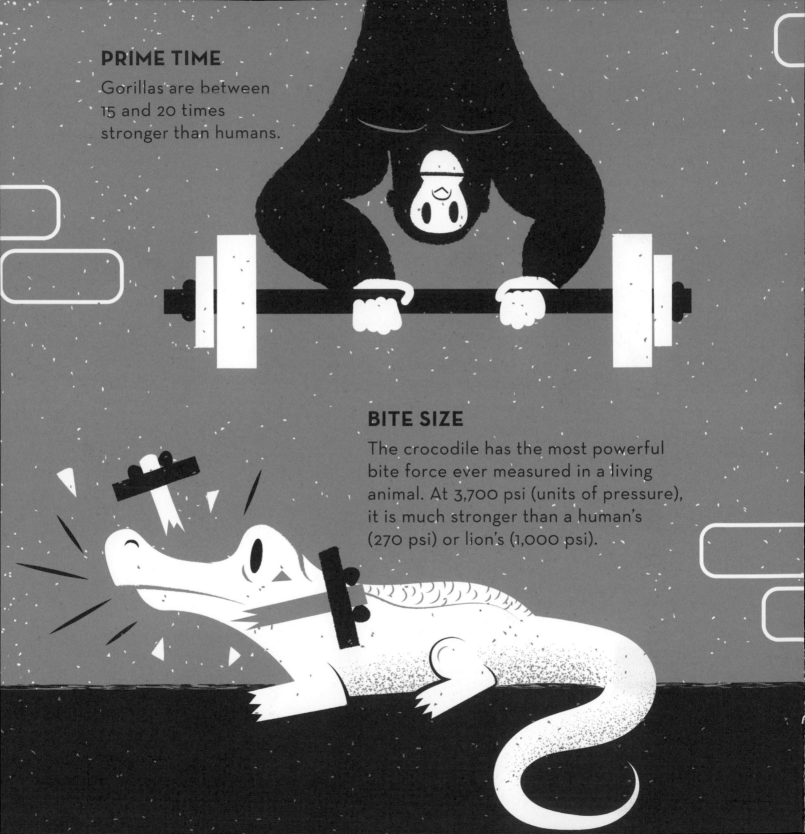

PRIME TIME

Gorillas are between 15 and 20 times stronger than humans.

BITE SIZE

The crocodile has the most powerful bite force ever measured in a living animal. At 3,700 psi (units of pressure), it is much stronger than a human's (270 psi) or lion's (1,000 psi).

BIG BIRD

The eagle is the mightiest bird in the world, able to lift prey that is four times its own weight.

STRONG BEETLE

The humble dung beetle is a champ. It is the strongest living creature on Earth. The male can pull 1,141 times its own bodyweight.

STERLING CHILDREN'S BOOKS
New York

An Imprint of Sterling Publishing Co., Inc.
1166 Avenue of the Americas
New York, NY 10036

ISBN 978-1-4549-3760-9
Distributed in Canada by Sterling Publishing Co., Inc.
c/o Canadian Manda Group, 664 Annette Street
Toronto, Ontario M6S 2C8, Canada
For information about custom editions, special sales, and premium and corporate purchases,
please contact Sterling Special Sales at 800-805-5489 or
specialsales@sterlingpublishing.com.
Manufactured in China
Lot #:
2 4 6 8 10 9 7 5 3 1
07/19
sterlingpublishing.com

OCT 2019